Little Heroes

A Story of Courage, Determination and Friendship

Princess

Honey

Rafael

Written by Nanci Ianzano

Illustrated by Marcos Salazar

Acknowledgements

Thank you Lee, Kristen, Cindy, Pat and John
for your encouragement.

Thank you Marcos for bringing *Little Heroes* to
life through your creative illustrations.

Dedication

For my little Princess

"Be who you are and say what you feel
because those who mind don't matter
and those who matter don't mind."

Dr. Seuss

Welcome To
Quiet Meadows

Down the road is a farm called Quiet Meadows.

Quiet Meadows
FARM STAND
home grown vegetables

There is much activity on the farm, with the farmer selling fruits and vegetables, collecting eggs from the chickens, bailing hay, and taking care of his animals.

There are three Mini Horses on the farm, Princess, Honey and Rafael, who are best friends. They play all day together in the field, jumping, running and having lots of fun. The Big Horses watch them play and think they're really silly.

They stretch their necks over the fence and say, "You are not real horses. You are all so little. You are too small to ride, or even do anything helpful on this farm."

Princess responds, "We may be small, but we can accomplish big things."

The Big Horses just whinny and gallop away, kicking dirt onto the three tiny horses.

Rafael turns to Princess and says,
"Why do you talk to those Big Horses?
They always laugh at us and call us names.
They make us feel sad and worthless."

Princess says, "Don't cry, those Big Horses don't know any better. They think we have no value because we are little. One day they will understand that we are all special and important in our own way."

Every night the farmer puts all the animals away for the evening.
Chickens go in the chicken coop.
Pigs go in their pen. The Big Horses go in their big barn. And the three Mini Horses go in their mini barn.

One night there was a terrible thunderstorm. The rain began to fall so hard that large puddles formed all over the farm.

The powerful wind caused the barn doors to rattle and shake, making all the animals very nervous and scared.

The chickens were clucking and flapping their wings, the pigs were squealing and snorting, and all the horses were whinnying and kicking.

Honey yelled,
  "That old oak tree is starting
to fall on the **Big Horse**
                    barn!"

Princess shouted,
  "We have to do something or
the Big Horses will be **trapped!**"

Rafael nervously cried,

"But we're so little...
what can we do?"

Princess responded, "I have an idea! Being little will help us because we can reach the latches on our stall doors to free ourselves."

Princess, Honey and Rafael leaned over
their doors and stretched their necks.
First, they had to open the latches
on their stalls.

With one strong YANK upward, they
got the latches to open and were FREE!

The three Mini Horses rushed out
together and headed toward the big barn.
The wind and rain sprayed their faces
and pushed them back.

They could hear the other animals on the farm making all kinds of frightening noises. The Mini Horses could see that the limbs on the oak tree were hanging low now. Rafael shouted, "It's going to BREAK. It's going to BREAK! We have to get out of here... FAST!"

Honey said, "It's up to us to free the Big Horses! We must work together as a team to do it!"

The three Mini Horses quickly ran to the barn, each one going to a different stall. The Big Horses were so scared as they looked down at the tiny faces.

Princess looked up and said "Don't worry, we are all here to help you!"

With that, they each stood on their hind legs as high as they could go. Stretching their necks and using their noses, they lifted the latches on the stall doors.

Just as the horses escaped, there was a loud SNAP. Then the oak tree came CRASHING down on top of the Big Horse barn.

The farmer came running out of his house.

"Oh no!" he shouted. "Look at my barn! Where are my horses?"

To his relief, all of the horses had escaped unharmed. They were all safe and huddled together in the open field.

The Big Horses looked down at Princess,
Honey and Rafael and said,
"We were mean and mistreated you.
We thought you had no
value because you were little... We were
wrong. Thank you for saving us.
You are our
Little Heroes!"

The three Mini Horses were happy
and whinnied, shaking their heads
in agreement.

Princess said,
"We will all be friends now."

And from that day on,
all the horses stayed
together in the big field,
playing, running and
eating the lush
green grass.

PRAISE FOR *LITTLE HEROES*

"We all recognize the value of social skills and are eager to teach and expose our children to an appropriate social/relational interplay. The story *Little Heroes* does precisely that. The frolicking, fun-loving little horses maintain their spirit of fun and camaraderie even as they are taunted and bullied by the larger, mean-spirited horses. In maintaining their unit in fostering kindness, the little horses end up as champions in the end. This is a story where kindness triumphs over bullying."

Celeste Mancinelli MS CCC SLP
Social Skills Instructor/Therapeutic Options

"The importance of self-esteem cannot be underestimated for people of any age, but it is particularly critical in the young. A sense of worth, value, and ability can determine a child's future long before they reach adulthood, becoming one of the key elements to either a lifetime of success or one of failure. What Nanci Ianzano is doing with *Little Heroes* is endowing children with a clear understanding that they all have strengths, they all therefore have something meaningful to offer the world, and that all lives matter. It is one of the most imperative and most powerful lessons we can pass to the next generation."

Wil Mara
Bestselling author of more than 150 books for children

About the Author

Nanci Ianzano retired from her career as a Speech/Language Specialist in Paterson, New Jersey, but continues to combine her love of working with children with her passion for animals. In this, her first children's book, three Mini Horses help teach a valuable lesson to the bullying Big Horses.

An inspiring story that hopefully will open conversations with elementary school children and adults about being confident and resourceful when confronted with harassment or intimidation.

Nanci's horses live on a beautiful farm in Newton, New Jersey, where they play all day with their friends and eat the lush green grass.

Contact the author at nianzano@yahoo.com

About the Illustrator

Of Dominican heritage, Marcos Salazar was born in the Bronx, New York, in 1993. He moved to Paterson, New Jersey, in 2011. As a young artist, he is constantly exploring the world around him. He often takes photographs of the places that interest him and uses the images as reference for his works of art.

From a sketch, the artist's imagination and emotions take over to create his artworks. Besides doing illustrations, Marcos is completing his Bachelor of Fine Art degree, with a concentration in painting.

Contact the illustrator at m.salazar.art@gmail.com

www.ingramcontent.com/pod-product-compliance
Lightning Source LLC
LaVergne TN
LVHW072120070426
835511LV00002B/40